ALL KINDS OF
SHIPS

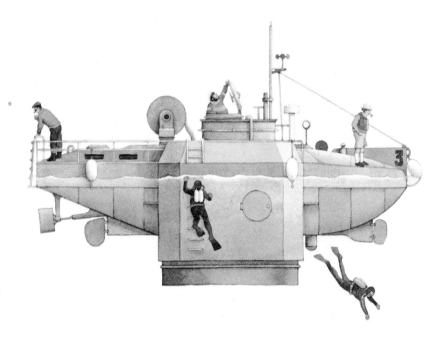

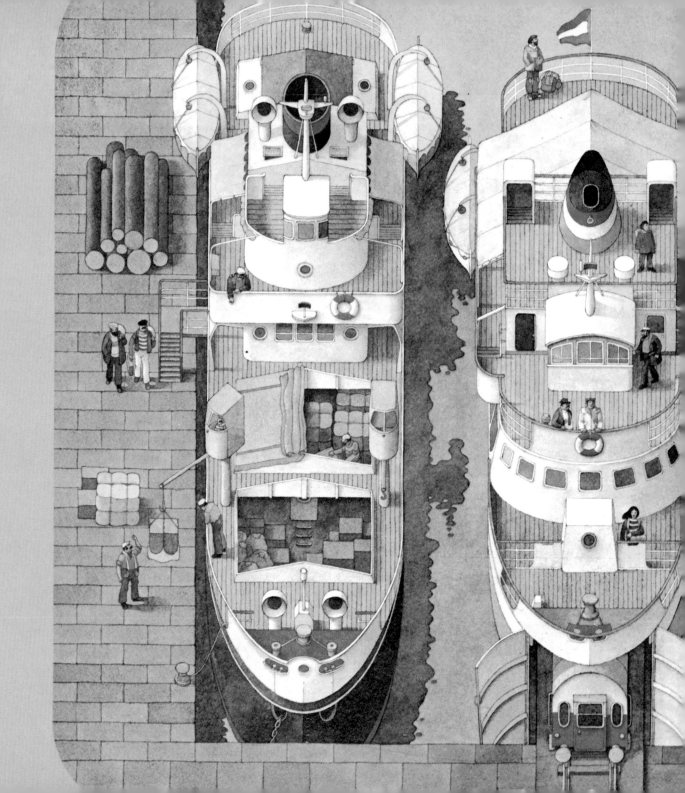

ALL KINDS OF SHIPS

By Seymour Reit

Pictures by
Roberto Innocenti

 Golden Press • New York
Western Publishing Company, Inc.
Racine, Wisconsin

Rocks and waterfalls were problems for early river sailors.

EARLY SHIPS

No one knows for sure, but the story of how ships were invented may go like this: Long, long ago, long before there were roads or trains or planes, a weary traveler was walking beside a river. Then a log floated by. The walker climbed onto the log, and rode the rest of the way home. This floating log was probably the very first "ship."

Later on people learned to hollow out the logs, so they could sit in them and paddle. Some early sailors tied logs together with vines to form rafts. Others made boats with the skin of a large animal. They stretched the skin over a frame of tree branches.

Early boats were made by chopping up the inside of a log with a stone ax. Boats made this way are called dugouts.

Next people put sails on their ships. When the wind blew, it filled the sails and pushed the ships. Early sailboats could only go in the direction in which the wind was blowing. And if the wind blew too hard, or not hard enough, or in the wrong direction, rowers went to work. Other people were needed to steer the ships.

As time passed, bigger ships were built and more sails were added. People studied the wind and placed the sails to catch every breeze. These bigger sailboats could travel on long voyages—even without the help of any rowers.

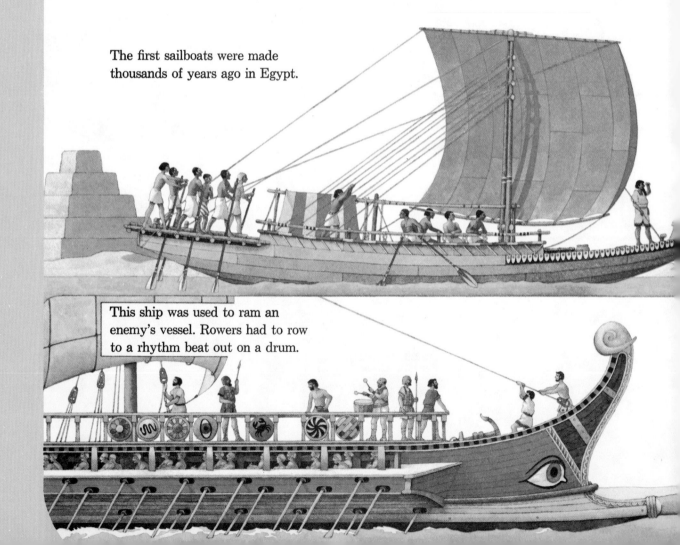

The first sailboats were made thousands of years ago in Egypt.

This ship was used to ram an enemy's vessel. Rowers had to row to a rhythm beat out on a drum.

The Vikings were expert sailors. They explored many lands. Some people think they discovered America before Columbus.

Columbus sailed for 2½ months to get from Europe to the Americas. His small wooden ship the *Santa Maria* looked like this.

Sailing warships had many decks, which bristled with cannons. In rough seas the lowest gunports were closed so water wouldn't flood the ship.

The *Mayflower* carried settlers to America. Its average speed was only 2 miles per hour. Most people walk faster than that!

Pirate ships prowled the seas hoping to capture vessels with valuable cargo. Sometimes the pirates sank a captured ship.

Sailing ships that were wide and bulky ruled the seas for hundreds of years. They were used to fight battles, explore unknown waters, and carry passengers and cargo all over the world.

Then a new kind of sailing ship came into use. It was long and narrow. It had taller masts with extra sails. It could speed through the waves much faster than the old-style ships. This new kind of ship was called a clipper ship. It was the fastest sailing ship ever made.

Graceful clipper ships sailed from America to faraway places like Australia and China. Their Captains took pride in setting new port-to-port speed records. The *Sea Witch* was a China clipper famous for swiftness.

Another fast sailing ship in the time of the clippers was the schooner. This one was nearly 400 feet long and had sails on 7 tall masts.

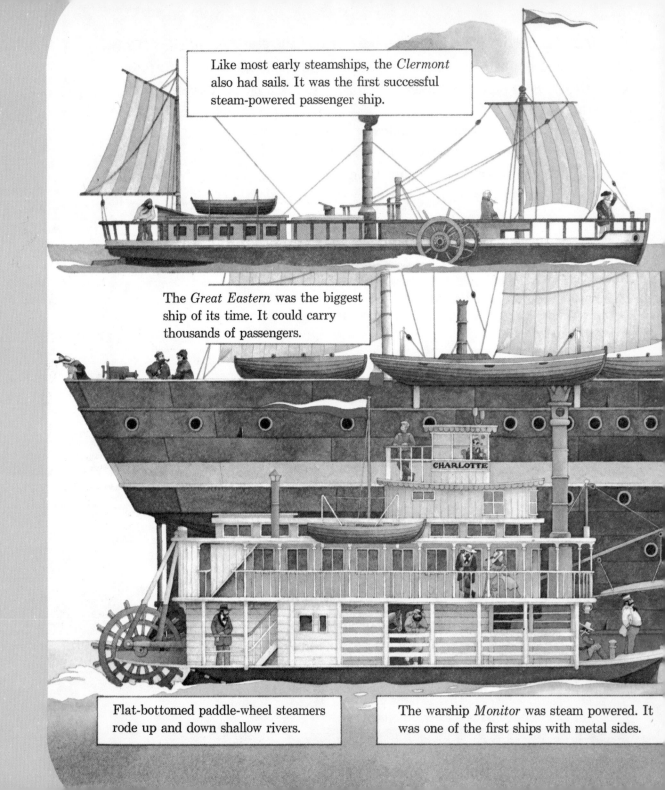

Like most early steamships, the *Clermont* also had sails. It was the first successful steam-powered passenger ship.

The *Great Eastern* was the biggest ship of its time. It could carry thousands of passengers.

CHARLOTTE

Flat-bottomed paddle-wheel steamers rode up and down shallow rivers.

The warship *Monitor* was steam powered. It was one of the first ships with metal sides.

America's first working steamboat was built in 1807 by Robert Fulton. In those days people laughed at the idea of steam engines for ships. Fulton named his vessel the *Clermont*, but everyone else called it "Fulton's Folly."

Ships powered by steam engines soon put the wind-powered sailing ships out of business. Steamships could travel faster than sailships, but more important, they could travel anytime. At long last sailors did not have to wait for the wind to blow. They went whenever they wanted—wind or no wind.

TODAY'S SHIPS

Today there are boats and ships of all shapes and sizes. They do many useful jobs. Some carry mail. Some, like ferryboats and ocean liners, carry passengers. Fishing boats bring in tons of fish to help feed people. Cargo ships and tankers go to distant ports to pick up or deliver many things people use every day, like cars and clothes and oil and oats.

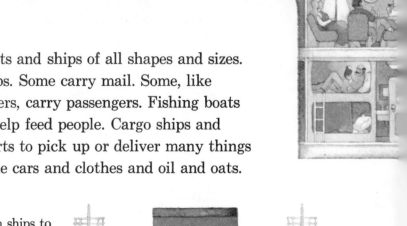

Dock cranes move cargo from ships to waiting railroad trains.

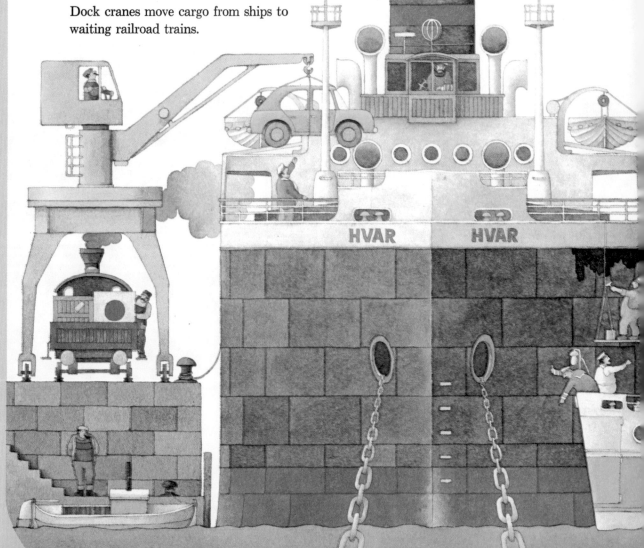

HVAR HVAR

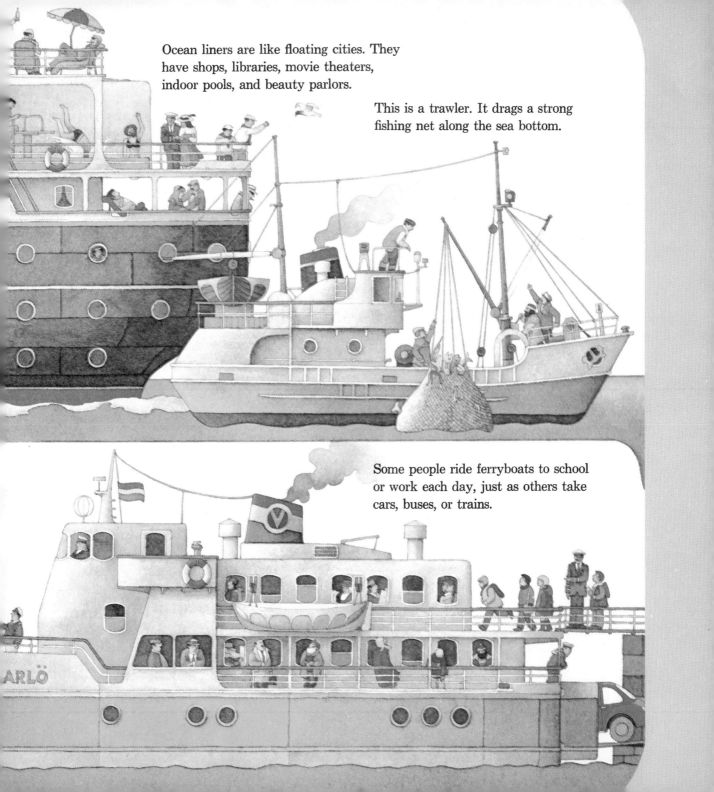

Ocean liners are like floating cities. They have shops, libraries, movie theaters, indoor pools, and beauty parlors.

This is a trawler. It drags a strong fishing net along the sea bottom.

Some people ride ferryboats to school or work each day, just as others take cars, buses, or trains.

ARLÖ

Lighthouses help ships find their way safely.
They are like traffic signs for water travelers.

passenger ship

patrol boat

ferryboat

fireboat

motorboat

HOTEL

A harbor is a busy place. And a crowded one. Passenger liners steam in after long ocean crossings. Ferryboats shuttle back and forth. Barges load and unload at piers. Fireboats, police boats, tugboats, and cargo ships are everywhere. All sailors have to learn special "traffic rules" of the sea. This makes water travel safer. Just think what harbor traffic jams there might be if sailors didn't have any "rules of the road"!

oil tanker

sailboat

cargo ship

barge

sight-seeing boat

tugboat

In some places people live year round on houseboats. They take their homes with them whenever they move.

SPECIAL SHIPS

Different parts of the world have their own special ships. In Venice, a city in Italy that has many canals, gondolas are pushed through the water with long poles. The people of the West Indies travel from one island to another in sturdy catamarans. The Eskimos of the Far North ride in special canoes called kayaks. Kayaks fit snugly around the rider's waist so the cold Arctic waters don't get in.

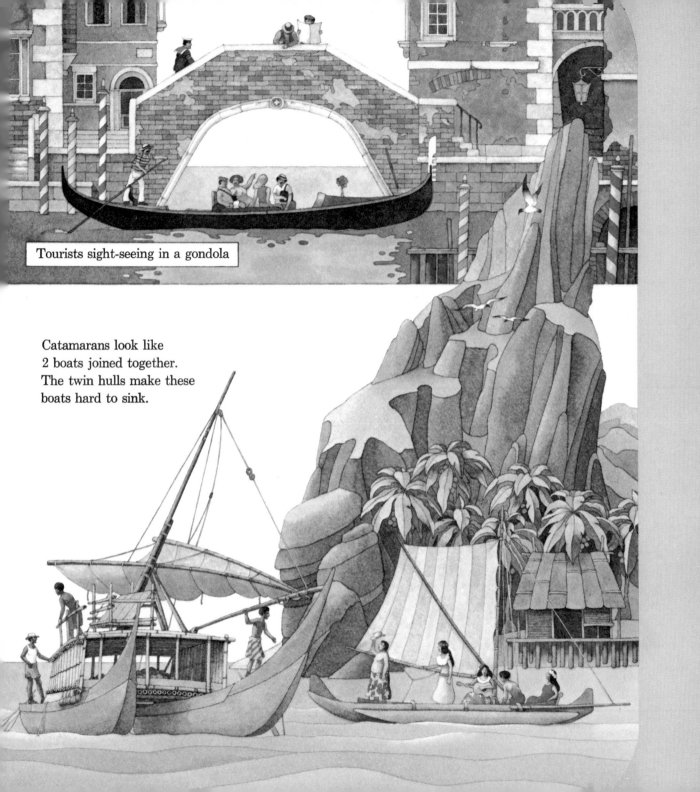

Tourists sight-seeing in a gondola

Catamarans look like
2 boats joined together.
The twin hulls make these
boats hard to sink.

Did you ever see a ship travel *above* the water?
The hovercraft does. It floats on a cushion of air.
Hydrofoils can also skim above the water's surface.
They speed along on metal fins.

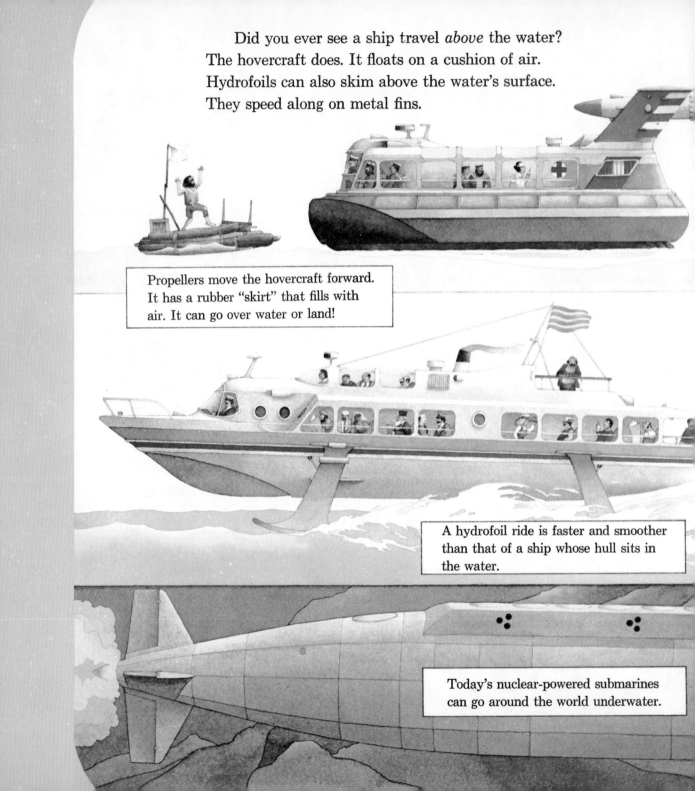

Propellers move the hovercraft forward.
It has a rubber "skirt" that fills with
air. It can go over water or land!

A hydrofoil ride is faster and smoother
than that of a ship whose hull sits in
the water.

Today's nuclear-powered submarines
can go around the world underwater.

Other ships move silently beneath the sea. In bathyspheres, bathyscaphes, and submarines, scientists study the dark and mysterious undersea world. With these ships people have been able to dive deep into places they've never seen before.

A bathysphere is attached by a cable to a surface ship. A bathyscaphe moves about under its own power.

America's first submarine could stay underwater half an hour. It was hand cranked by a single crew member.

Rushing the white-water rapids in kayaks

Iceboating on a frozen lake

Many boats are just for fun and sport. Water skiers are pulled by fast motorboats. Snorkelers and skin divers use boats to take them to coral reefs. Racers compete in speedboats and sailboats. Campers enjoy canoe trips. And some people like rowboats for just sitting and bobbing lazily up and down in the waves.

Fishing from a rowboat or paddling in a canoe is fun to do with friends.

Racing the wind in a sleek speedboat

Relaxing on board a yacht

Sailing in a strong breeze takes skill.

Viewing the undersea world —and being viewed

NEPTUNE II

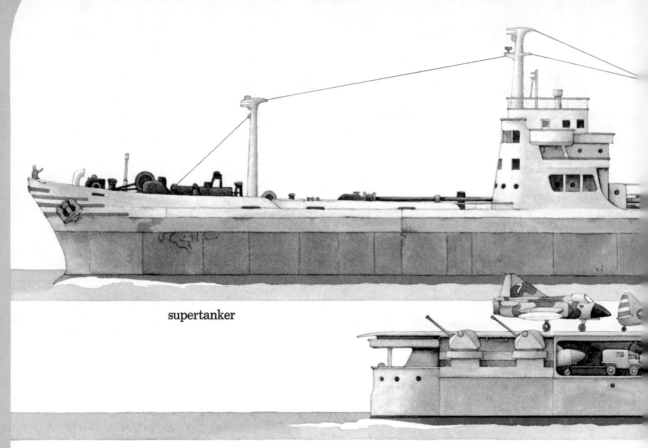

supertanker

aircraft carrier

WE'VE COME A LONG WAY

People and ships have changed a lot since the first floating log was ridden down a river. We have gone from crude rafts to modern hovercrafts, from tiny sailing ships to huge aircraft carriers, from slow paddleboats to speedy ocean liners.

It's hard to imagine that ships will ever be better than the ones we have today. But the people in Columbus' time may have thought the same thing, and just look how far ships have come since then!

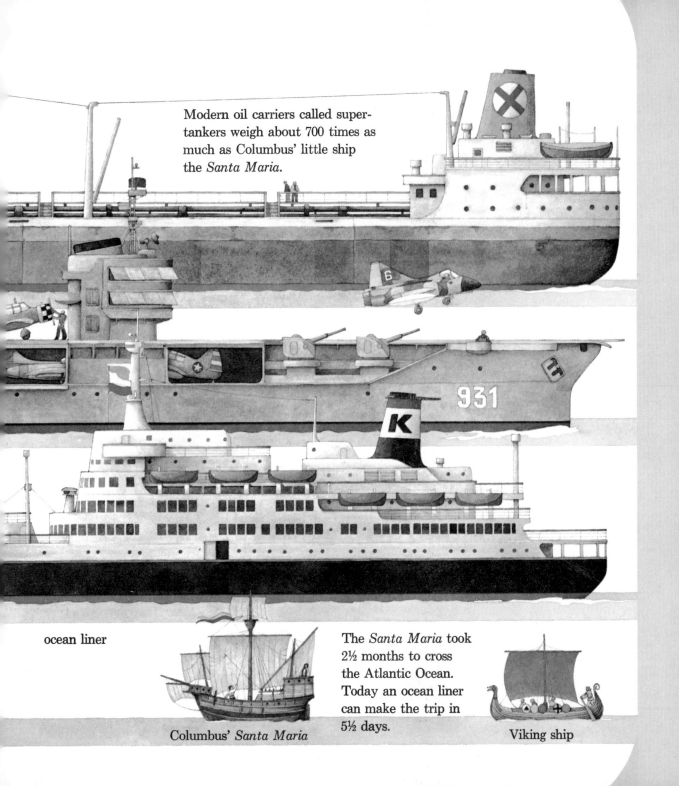

Modern oil carriers called super-tankers weigh about 700 times as much as Columbus' little ship the *Santa Maria*.

ocean liner

The *Santa Maria* took 2½ months to cross the Atlantic Ocean. Today an ocean liner can make the trip in 5½ days.

Columbus' *Santa Maria*

Viking ship